THE
TUTANKHAMUN
VARIATIONS

›THE‹
TUTANKHAMUN
VARIATIONS

JOHN GREENING

BLOODAXE BOOKS

Copyright © John Greening 1984, 1991

ISBN: 1 85224 104 7

First published 1991 by
Bloodaxe Books Ltd,
P.O. Box 1SN,
Newcastle upon Tyne NE99 1SN.

Bloodaxe Books Ltd acknowledges
the financial assistance of Northern Arts.

Cover reproduction by V & H Reprographics, Newcastle upon Tyne.

Typesetting by Bryan Williamson, Darwen, Lancashire.

Printed in Great Britain by
Bell & Bain Limited, Glasgow, Scotland.

To Stuart Henson

Acknowledgements

Acknowledgements are due to the editors of the following publications in which some of these poems first appeared: *Encounter, Orbis, Other Poetry, Outposts, Oxford Poetry, Poetry Durham, Poetry Review, Poetry with an Edge* (Bloodaxe Books, 1988), *Prospice, The Rialto, Stand, Verse,* and *The World & I* (Washington Times Corporation, USA). '1972' was broadcast on *Poetry Now* (BBC Radio 3) under the title 'The Treasures of Tutankhamun'.

The Winter Journey is based on a journey undertaken in 1911 when three members of Scott's Antarctic expedition went to collect an Emperor Penguin's egg. It was first published in John Greening's pamphlet *Winter Journeys* (Rivelin Press, 1984).

Contents

THE
TUTANKHAMUN
VARIATIONS

Carter at Swaffham

We know him: it's
the Carter lad who
painted dear Lady
Amherst's lap-dog

and the Vicar's old
bull-terrier, quite
without schooling – son
of our gamekeeper's son.

And if his imagination
pierces a tiny hole
in these venerable walls
and holds a candle

through to a room full
of wonderful things
but utterly foreign to
a decorously mounted

hunting party with
its fine equipage,
its whips and sticks and
stuccoed wooden courtesy –

then what is that to us?
Tally-ho! and on towards
the twentieth century: let
the boy be content

with keeping trespassers
from our noble pile;
or immortalise our
ailing Golden Retrievers.

Chorus of Newsmen

We are looking for a story.
A running story, like the war.
But not the war.
An English story.
Like Jack the Ripper.
Like the Titanic.
Like Scott of the Antarctic.
We miss the hot lead
We used to catch.
We miss those fat statistics
That used to cover our front pages.
We can do nothing with this
Latest dance, that latest creation.
We are ready to jump into an aeroplane
And leave for any part of the globe.
(What is that Messenger carrying
So swiftly from Dover?)
We need a story.
(Who is that recluse reminiscing
Amid the cigar smoke?)
We need a story.
(And what is being unsealed?
And why that smile?
And whose are the words on that telegram?)
We are looking for a story
For the aristocracy at breakfast,
For the middle classes on the train,
For the working-man on the street corner.
(And why has the Editor of the *Times*
Gone to Newbury Races?)
Something to do with money.
One story that is a total
Eclipse of the sun and will last
Until the next war.
Something to do with death.
(And why has the Earl of Carnarvon
Cancelled all his engagements?)
Something to do with mystery.

We are looking for a story
That will set the peace ablaze.
A story that is not a question.
Not Irish.
And not emancipated women.
But which can be embroidered
And photographed and sold.
(Where is that young man hurrying
With his notebook?)
And not the civil war in China.
(What is that noise in the telegraph wires?)
And not the riots in Egypt.

1914

The landscape overhead will not be changed
By flash-flood: it is a civilisation
Bunkered securely in its desolation.
More admirable, too, than this gold arranged
About my sarcophagus – hanging its strange
Treasures freely on view, a virgin cache
Unnoticed by the lords whose liberation
From dirty politics is a trench
In the Kings' Valley. I warned them to keep
Their distance from this entrance and its seal.
Anubis is no god, but a dog asleep,
So let him lie. Small punctures may heal
Once you've unmuzzled him; but not (that steep
Descent over) your mad desire to steal.

Theodore Davis's Last Season

I have dug for treasure the way I smoke –
without stopping, and obsessively.

If I could have made my fortune
like one Mr Standwood of Maine,

who imported mummies by the ton
to turn into brown wrapping paper,

then I would have saved myself twelve
years of sweat. Or if I had been alive

the century before him, I should have
ground up the flesh and sold it

to the poor at an immense profit.
But no one today is after mummy-powder.

If I surrender this choice concession,
then that pariah dog Carnarvon will be down

scratching where I've been, although he knows
I have already published Touatankhamanou.

It's only this old seductress on my desk,
this strange alluring figurine –

and when I hear her boyish voice, 'the best
is yet...' I should know it's time to quit:

she has promised me into too many dark
and secret hollows, whispering 'intact'...

I shall return to Florida, and make sure
I die before she can call back: 'See? I promised!'

1972

I am waiting, like all the others, waiting
To open the sacred seal and discover
My future; and as I wait, this exhibition
Snakes me through steel barriers to my golden
Eighteenth year where I catch, amid the darkness
That enfolds a teenage Pharaoh's history,

Glimmerings of a more personal history,
As if it had lain beneath the sand waiting
For me to come and dig into its darkness
In search of the famous Mask but discover
Only in each glass case my own face, golden.
It is my coming-of-age exhibition.

All aspects of me are in this exhibition:
The child's chair and board-game are a history
Of my early youth; my teens were that golden
Dagger. This trumpet, this cow-bed are waiting
For me to experiment, to discover
In their cross-meshed passages of darkness,

In sexual unity and divine darkness,
The Goddess Hathor's milk-white exhibition
Of her transfiguring powers: discover
Between her lyriform horns all history.
The Necklace of the Rising Sun is waiting
To embrace us, its clasp is cool and golden...

Each morning my hopes shoot greener, but golden
Futures only bloom after months in darkness,
During nights of counting the weeks of waiting,
And now at this jubilee exhibition
I am persuaded that time and history
Are relative. Come, UCCA! and discover

To me the sacred light, let us discover
The place where we are to spend our golden
Prime and inscribe our names on history,
As one young man did, emerging from darkness
At eighteen to become this exhibition –
The very thing for which we are all waiting.

The Cedars at Highclere

I see him in the distance. The stories he tells them
waft across to me as I trim the lawns beneath his cedars.

He loves cedars: his father asked my father to put them in.
The Egyptians made all their tables and chairs out of cedar,

he told me once, were buried surrounded by it. Now he's
alone on that fancy verandah, reading, or glancing up towards

these living crowns – always some fat volume open beside him.
That's (he'd say) since forty days stuck out in tropical seas

with so little to do, between fighting off pirates
and avoiding hurricanes, that he fell prey to the bookworm.

But we know. In the old days he would never have stopped
still long enough to have turned a leaf. If it wasn't the sea,

it was the turf; if it wasn't the latest horseless carriage,
it was some infernal air machine. Faster, always faster, until

Trotman comes running to pluck him out from that blazing wreck
in the Black Forest – head smashed, heart stopped.

And all he wanted to know was had he killed anybody!
Next thing, he is making Highclere a home for war-wounded,

young lads cowering behind this shadow-line: muttering, wide-eyed
ghost battalions. M'lord was never one to let the grass grow.

Today he showed us another of his latest photographs – one of
a mummified cat, which wasn't at all well received by his dog –

nor by her Ladyship, for that matter. But then, we all have doubts
about this digging up of times long gone. The papers make jokes

about the thousands he has wasted (with 36,000 acres
here to keep) and to my own thinking, when there's talk of a curse

you think twice. He's already had a good nine lives – chased
by a wild elephant in South Africa (more of an achievement

to have escaped than shot it, he said!), then only last week
rushed to the hospital with three quarters of an hour to live.

When he dies, it will be in a way nobody could have foreseen.
'I don't think I've lost my nerve,' he whispered, straight

after that accident. And he won't let anyone wrap him up
in bandages. 'I want to be buried,' he laughs, 'out in the open,

high up on Beacon Hill, then – if you like –' to us, he calls us
his garden angels! – 'plant one of de Havilland's DH9s

above me like a Pyramid; and make sure the grave is dug
by a professional archaeologist!' Tomorrow he's off out

to the East again. The last season, he has announced.
'If the Pharaohs don't bite, the mosquitoes certainly will.'

Carter Begins

I

There is a language of rock that is not
like the language of diplomacy

or newspapers or love. One must know
how to read it, where to begin. None of us

has heard it spoken, though some taste the air
into which its last words evaporated,

a few have grovelled to wrench gold fillings
from its mouth. There is a grammar of rock,

but its secrets are guarded by aloof
priestesses, their fingers to their lips as they

scald meaning from the bones. I will begin
with a triangle I know to mean hope.

Aboard the *Champollion*, steaming
towards the Pharos, unknown, unrecognised,

I imagine steps that lead into chambers
full of the poetry of this rock language.

II

The Valley in which we search
fruitlessly is peaceful:

we dream of gardens or of
a golden age, and our looking

is contented. If we knew what
sentences of hard labour

await us the day we crack
the dream, we would not know

this pleasure, sipping at
perhaps and may, shifting

ten thousand irritations
at a stroke. But the demons

of discovery are less
considerate – they will block-

book the hotels, and arrive
each morning in dark glasses,

rattling metal plates,
begging their thousand words.

III

Down to bedrock now – but
all we have to show is

thirteen jars containing
the remains of sweet oils

used to anoint the dead.
Lady Carnarvon stoops

and for an instant glows
pre-Raphaelite again:

Miss Almina Wombwell
delivering the first

flush of her youth into
her lover's arms. Is this

a final remembrance
of 'that night devoted

to oils, when thou art re-
united with the earth'?

Now she kneels to a lost
fragrance, alabaster

jars look pale disciples;
and we – two wretched thieves

mocked and left here to parch
with a mystery king.

Entr'acte

Some friendships fell apart
when they met our English
damp. Some were too
delicate to have been carried
out of the past. Perhaps
others will be reclaimed and
restored. Two sentinels
remain standing:

                       Stuart,
you were as watchful and all-
seeing with your one eye
as Ra, ever-forgiving
when we forgot and threw
the old washing-up sock
for you to catch; breaking
into your native Welsh in
the *souk*, or kick-starting
a rustic Arabic which you had
patched up until it could
drive a class of sixty to
drill out, 'I'm-fine-thanks!'
to your every 'How are you?'
And how you hated that head-
mistress of ours (whose name
meant 'tin can', and whose face
resembled one) for wagging
a finger at you when you tried
to "borrow" one of her clutch
of Louis Quatorze to stock
our chairless staff-room.
You could bellow your own
Son-et-Lumière when you wanted
to get things done your way;
or simply sat with your shoe-
soles turned insultingly
on your victim. 'A fox!'
as our idiom-proud Inspector
of English chuckled. Yes –
and a superb actor to that last

20

encore when you soliloquised
draconian indignation before a
baffled policeman. Scene:
the Pyramids. To be or
not to be arrested on your
last day in Egypt. Always making
new friends and taking us
on sightseeing marathons through
backstreet dust-bowls and
open sewers to try a glass of
sugared tea and *bassboussa* –
to meet Abdul Kareem, black
and glistening on the desert's rim
in a mud-brick storage-heater,
whose latrine ran cockroaches,
and whose library lacked only
Volume Two of *Lives of the Poets* –
to meet Mr Sami and his Violet,
who fish-fed us and let us
bloat on their privileged panorama
of the Nile and Sadat being
bulleted past, as they put in
their requests for Macleans tooth-
paste, Marks & Spencer shirts...
then merrily bolted the door
to show us the strength of
their hospitality – Stuart,
you tolerated it all, even
when Alan popped up, dear
utterly-different-from-you old
Alan, whose cracked earthenware
humour could keep even his own
temper cool. Who else
would try to tell the joke
about a whisky and a white
horse called Eric to a room
full of Moslem Brothers?
Or endlessly repeat the story
of how he slid down into
that camel's ball-cracking jaws
such that I can still smell its
eunuch-making snorts today?
Alan, we miss you falling off

your bike, and holding forth
on hieroglyphs and syntax
and black kites, or blundering
into arguments with jumped-up
officialdom and market-sharks
and little horrors and bigwigs
and Jane. Even Jane (like the frogs
who used to rev-rev as you sang)
misses your crooning choruses –
'Beware of Long Lankin...'
Beware all those unmarried girl
students gazing at you from inside
their Dalek costumes. 'Will you
allow me to come in?' you made
them repeat if they were late.
Task-master! And Asmi,
our old laundry man, he misses
your Nile-smooth conversations
up on that scorching roof above
the domino slaps, *sheesha*
fumes and warbling wailing cassette
drone of the café. And Ahmed,
our Professor of Physics,
misses those searching debates
about the possibility and
necessity of classrooms, about
the ultimate origin of
our pay-packets...

                          Alan
and Stuart, you were
two golden companions during
our year of prospecting for
poverty, and still you are –
despite that a-hundred-and-
twenty-degree day out when
you had cycled on ahead up
the white mountain to reach
the Valley of the Kings
well before us, unthinkingly
bearing away the Greenings'
unique and most precious
yellow water bottle.

Water Boy

Is the lad who breezes here on the sun's first ray,
Who brings water to the men, who watches motionless
The excavation mound while they ablute and pray,

The genie who – civilisations ago – rolled a grey
Pitcher above the Valley and watched it smash its torrent
Down into the Place of Truth, sweeping away

All entrances to the Old Kingdom? Because today
That boy took a stick in his hand and, with motions
Like a water-diviner, revealed where a king lay.

November 4th

At home, the leaves
will by now have turned,
and the small boys

cart from doorstep
to foggy doorstep
masked pyjamas full

of the *Daily News*,
croaking: 'Penny
for the Guy, guv?'

But here the sand
is already ablaze,
and that momentary

crackle under the
soul, that brief
flash from my boyhood,

is smothered by
this day's ambitions.
The morning is on

a blue fuse and
the men are
standing clear.

Silently they nod
to where a small boy
awaits me on the step

he has unearthed.
(Penny for a
Golden Rain, guv?)

Opening

A cache of
aristocrats
unearthed by the
Antiquities Department
watches Carter lift
the crowbar
   ('We're going to have
   a concert!'
   winks Carnarvon)
and break into
the sealed
burial chamber.

Two have already
been in here
unofficially once
but disguised their
entry and withdrawal
with a pile of reeds
and a Moses basket
   ('left by the tomb-
   robbers in their
   haste...')
and now
at all costs
they must pretend
that they are seeing
everything for
the first time.
   ('Carter's going to
   sing a song!')

The alabaster lamp
seems to writhe
and croon, its limbs
a triple lotus
growing from a sacred pond
like the legs and welcoming

arms of a cabaret star
that single you out
and usher you in
and show you the circle
which you must enter
before you may open the shrine.

The spectators
will the two
protagonists
to speak
to elaborate...

but they stand,
a momentary shudder
of guilt shadowing
the triumphant
backdrop of gold and blue

and suddenly –
not words, no words
from this dumbstruck
double-act

but a whisper
from the black wings
from a small lamp
with a wick
and a mud base:

It is I
who hinder
the sand
from choking
the secret
chamber

I am for
the protection
of the deceased

26

Sir John Maxwell Nearly Comes to Grief
in a Luxor Street, February 1923...

'I am an Englishman! and Chairman
of the Egyptian Exploration Fund!'

he shouted, but the boy
and his demon dog-cart had
vanished.

          Upon being visited
by the Police Chief of Luxor,
the father (only possessor
of a dog-cart in that city)
was persuaded to thrash his son
to within an inch of his life
and to donate ten pounds,
to be distributed from the gates
of the Winter Palace in the name
of Sir John Maxwell, to the poor –

who were most grateful
to the boy.

The Picnic

You've not been down yet?
Sir Arthur assures me
it's nothing so very
exciting. We've been here
an hour, and all we've seen
is one ancient native
carrying out something
most unpleasant wrapped up
in bandages. I've been
watching that odd young man
who's blind or has some strange
disability. You remember
Victor, of course. Last
year he took me to the Somme
and we had a splendid picnic
in one of the trenches – yes,
they were my feelings too,
absolutely – but we used
an old ammunition box for
a table and it was perfectly
civilised. Then the darling
found me some pieces of
an old shell of ours and had it
made into a bracelet. Look
at that brazen flapper
powdering her nose! I do
hope we manage to take
home some little souvenir:
Victor has asked Lord Allenby.
You'll be at the rag-time
ball? Or do you agree that
there really are far too many
Americans? Oh quite!
Luxor would be divine
if it weren't for this
thoroughly gloomy business.

Carter's Dream

folding doors
with ebony bolts
in copper staples

opening on to
folding doors
with ebony bolts

and a clay seal
of the necropolis
opening on to

folding doors of
gilt tightly
bolted

and on a
knotted cord
the jackal

I run
folding doors
of intense gilt

doors getting
smaller gilt
blinding

A Pocket Collection

I

Touch these bright bead
sandals and their pattern
rolls for ever out of reach.

II

Grasshopper that hopped
from tomb to top pocket
to New York Art Dealer.

III

The King's Wishing Cup, found
too late for him to wish
to be left in peace.

The Unborn

Why did you turn away
from your friend when
he kissed his daughter,

and pretend to examine
this small black box?
And when it fell open,

why did your eyes take on
that peculiar brightness
as you saw (unexpectedly)

a pair of little coffins
side by side, head
to foot, inscribed

'Osiris', with no other
name; and in each coffin
a tinier one, of gold,

containing two unborn
and unidentified babies,
mummified and motherless,

one in a burial mask
pathetically huge
for its age? Are these

the children that you
did not have, that you
could not permit

into your life, 'too
busy with scientific
work', cataloguing

your Pharaoh's collection
of games and toys,
or trying to purloin

that lotus head,
cute and irresistible
as a first-born?

Visit of the Egyptian Antiquities Department's Inventory Commission

Each item labelled and in its own place.
The work (they had to admit) of a true
Professional. Just one final check through
Those storage boxes at the back. No trace
Of anything improper: only a case
From Fortnums, marked 'Best Claret'...Allah! a new
Baby lifted into the room! A blue
Sacred lotus blossom – the Sun God's face!

'I do not condemn you. It was a crime
Of passion. You will be dealt no punishment
By me – but by the Future. When the time
To weigh your heart nears, should my head prevent
The scales balancing, you may have to climb
And be questioned by her correspondent.'

Lifting the Lid

Lifting the lid on our
uncertain longing
for a god –

these ropes and pulleys
are the liturgy
of modern belief,

but no explanation of
darkness can
be found in the light –

when you touch your
own hand in the mirror,
what you feel is glass.

B

Carter's Descent
(February 1924)

To come down these sixteen steps
holding the keys, the sole keys,
and hearing the reverberation from
that heavy iron grille; to know
that not even the *Times* correspondent
can follow me here...
                        To come down
and enter the darkness and to see
through the darkness a cracked lid
still suspended above that
most public, most secret mask, not
shaped to reflect either the lunacy
of a heretic predecessor or a star-
blind sacerdotage, but to glow
below the horizon of the sun-disc
modestly – no papyri, no press!...

To come down where everyone has appeared
to understand why their hands must be tied,
their heads bowed, their tongues slit –
why everything (chariot, ostrich feather
fan, mere child's toy) must be restrung
along my endless, exact, but unbreakable lines...

To come down where I have felt
alive and in command as if
it had been my own kingdom and I
liberated from fake courtesies
(permission denied/permission granted),
gilded wooden minds, hollow talkers...

To come down and handle a reed basket
of three thousand years ago, and forget
the three thousand unanswered letters
in my identical basket –

                        'Surely you must be
our long lost cousin from Camberwell...?
Might this perhaps cast light on the crisis

in the Congo...? Just send me a gold bar
or two – some mummy cloth – some of the beer
dregs – a grain of sand – I enclose half
a crown...'

                              To come down
to where the responsibility and the doubt
do not hang on their frayed ropes
like halves of that granite lid
cracked by a priest's men in antiquity,
lifted through the power of the English aristocracy,
abandoned to a rotten Egyptian bureaucracy...

Carnarvon – you would have smiled,
you would have gone out and shot a few hundred
rabbits or opened a magnum and toasted one
of two kings, or rested on this barbaric couch
before hurrying down to your beloved darkroom...

Carnarvon – your dog, your favourite dog,
howled and died with all the lights of Cairo
that April morning...
but the high, clear air of Beacon Hill
was golden, as they buried you, with lark song.

At noon, under the desert sun, I discover
steps that lead deep into myself.

To come down to this dark
and to know that after the long
bolero brays its climax
and the final veil of bullion
has been lifted, there will be sudden
leather and tooth and rag,
and the same bejewelled ignorance
as when we began –

                         is to come down
to earth, is to come down
to brass tacks, is to come down
carrying heavy iron keys
and to leave with a glimpse
of the golden ankh.

Abdul Ali and the Golden Bird

I

He tell me I have honest face, and say
I work for him – cook food – clean all his thing.
If work like donkey, he give much good pay.
So while he hunt for gold in tomb of king,
I hope for big reward. But he just bring
Canary in a cage. I say, 'Mabrook –
This bird of gold – it buy us both good luck!'

II

One week go by and he is dig up tomb.
I smile, 'We call this *Tomb of Golden Bird!*'
But he say, 'Empty word!', and leave his room
To Oostez Pecky, then go meet great Lord.
I ask this Pecky: 'When my big reward?'
But he just laugh, touch nose, and whisper me,
'You still have much to learn, Abdul Ali.'

III

It afternoon. All West Bank taking rest.
Then – much *kalaam* from Oostez Carter's door.
When people come find out, see one new guest.
Canary sing his good luck song no more:
But cobra – very dangerous snake – on floor.
And feathers. I tell them I asleep in bed.
I tell them cobra come from Pharaoh's head.

Copy
(for Miles)

To labour
for years
trying to dig
up the right
words to
sell Benson
and Hedges
Gold

      only
to see here
in their gold
canopic pack
the blackened
remains of
two King-
size lungs.

The Day I Found King Tut

Opposite the British Museum
just along from Coptic Street
is Davenports,
the magicians' shop.

I used to get their catalogue
sent and crept nightly
into the treasury:
fans, flowers, Floating

Zombies, Find the Lady,
Funny Bunny, Indian
Rope-trick, Chinese Rings –
and on the back page

all I could afford,
the after-dinner jokes –
a blue plastic coffin
with a red plastic

'King Tut' lying
quite snugly, held
by a concealed magnet,
which, with a sleight

of hand, you could
dislodge so that
like-poles repelled
and the Pharaoh would

not lie down, would
not lie down, only
you the arrogant
thirteen-year-old

knew how! I was
a regular mummy's
curse from the day
I found King Tut.

For My Father

March, 1923: now the sealed door
Is opened in the Valley of the Tombs
Of the Kings; and in Chiswick, you are born –
Not to a blaze of flash photography,
But crawling the width of a no-man's-land
Between two wars. Nor will you be brought up
Like a king, but by the time you are eighteen
Know the riches of possessing a bike
And wireless. No time for ancient history!
When you join up, you are delivered into
A modern, disarmingly naïve land,
So new it still bubbles. In Akureyri,
Your headset is picking up hieroglyphs,
But nothing, no greeting, from The Black Land
Or Living-Image-of-the-Hidden-One,
That eighteen-year-old with whom you share
A birthday; and it will be forty years
Before you feel you can make contact with
Your contemporary.

                           But by the time
We were pedalling into El Gurnah (famous
For its bandits) past squatting black covens
Of women, their sons like huge weathered masts
White lateen-sailed, your 7 a.m. breakfast
Had risen to 12 noon, and we panicked
Because of your diabetes. Semi-
Conscious, slumped there beside a drainage ditch
In a field of sugar, the sugar-carts
Swishing past, unrefined wallads flicking
The flies away and chewing lengths of cane,
You had regressed to the nineteen-twenties:
When (from that tomb-robbing Gurnah clan) down
Came a stranger, who climbed out of his taxi
And silently removed you to his house,
No rock chamber in the foothills, no cache
Of Middle Kingdom murals, but a simple
White-washed tunnel-vaulted house of mud brick
There on the fertile plain. Nor was his wife

Laden with stolen Pharaonic jewellery,
But brought us refreshing hibiscus juice,
And led you to lie beneath the cool vault
Of an empty bedroom.

                              Apart from the curse
Of disease, I don't believe in curses:
Although it was you who first directed me
To the dog that died, the lights that failed,
And Weigall's prophetic, 'Well, if he goes
Down the tomb in that spirit, I give him
Six weeks to live!' But I do remember
That your recovery seemed miraculous,
And when, the day after, you felt quite able
To walk down those sixteen steps, sixty years
Of Tutankhamun seemed inconsequential.

PLANTAGENETS

(to the memory of Philip Armitage)

For our own past is covered by the currents of action,
But the torment of others remains an experience
Unqualified, unworn by subsequent attrition.

T.S. ELIOT
The Dry Salvages

Richard I

Saladin sends me
more fresh chickens
to feed the hawk

he has heard I take
such risks
in keeping here.

He understands
that the man
possessing a lion's heart

must own all other parts
appropriate to a lion,
and that I do not

hunger only
after the cold sepulchre
of Jerusalem,

but worship each
of these warm
gifts he has sent

to me, their flesh
so maddeningly
sweet that

my physicians
advise me
I should not indulge.

Yes I am sick –
but sickness is all
I have ever enjoyed

since first I
leant crookedly on
my pilgrim staff

and felt it snap
under me,
or since the night

came muttering
how the King should
put away

all unlawful deeds
and beware
the Fate of Sodom.

I have become
like an *Assassin*,
drugged, lured

into The Old Man
of the Mountain's false
paradise, to try

the most smooth-skinned
soft, ripe,
and luscious-tasting

of his promises:
that after death
there will be no hood

on the instinct,
no curb
to the desires.

O Saladin,
I desire you
to send me no more

heathen street-fowl,
but fruit and snow only,
fresh fruit, fresh snow.

King John Crosses the Wellstream

Dysentery was our only chance.
So long as he had to keep dismounting

for a squat, we'd not lose track of him,
although the Fens kept trying

to draw a mist between us as we were hauling
his baggage-train from King's Lynn

through Wisbech towards the Wellstream.
But then, at the Estuary, the air

became as clear as that cut topaz
Pope Innocent gave to him, and at once

we knew that his sickness had lifted
along with the autumnal murk.

He breathed, looked north, and
said not a word (not even: were

his treasures all secure, his crosses,
his cups, his pearl-studded knife?) and

cracking another raw egg, beckoned
us on into the landscape's open mouth.

We heard the quicksand smacking its lips,
and the tide-rip's slobber; but he

was away off on the scent of cider,
swallowing his eggs whole, like a skua-gull.

Of the one hundred and forty-three cups
of white silver we have now emptied

into the darkening Wash, of the gold plates,
and of the crowns that have sunk like flatfish,

had he observed but one, or seen us attack
the thick cords binding his precious collection

of baths, valuing only – among the emeralds
and sapphires of the advancing tide –

a few more seconds gained, and up to our waists
and feeling the rear axle lurch,

had he but noticed our desperate tableau,
these fingers clutching the setting

shafts of his last pageant-cart,
and felt not hunger, not parricidal anger...

But King John is in Swineshead now, exultant
no doubt, and panting praises at his

deliverance from the gut-ache, enjoying
a ripe peach, the first of the new cider,

assuming that one of his servants will be on hand
to bring him the crown jewels to finger,

and his favourite bath, with kingly quantities
of healing water from the Wellstream.

Edward I

He had been playing chess.
With whom?
Toom Tabard, perhaps –
King Nobody!

But he had got up
to pace the room,
when from that shadowy
and uncharted area
above him,
from that high vaulting,
a clan of ancestral granite
came humbling down
on to his chair.

He had been about
to declare the game
a stalemate.

But instead, he
swept north
to Dunbar and
the Palace of Scone:

there claimed,
in case it should one
day fall
and crush the English throne,
the stone
that was a nation's destiny.

Edward II

It was to Berkeley Castle that they brought
Him after they had beaten him, hoping to
Starve him, and when he wouldn't be starved,

Inserted into his rectum a red-
Hot, specially procured, ox-roasting
Spit, that his body should not bear any mark.

Indeed it did not. But what remains of him,
His effigy, has been so scratched, scored with
Such viciousness, that all you can see is

I.H. pleading from the blank eyes, while his
Hair twists and snakes in supplication –
Smoke from an inextinguishable wrong.

The Black Prince

From Crécy, from Poitiers,
the bundles come, and
from each hops the Plague.

It bursts out in swellings
of pride, tongues that swing
deliriously in the church towers,

fountains that spew red wine,
and all the fascias
blotched with tapestry.

Gold cups from Gascony, rings,
coins, chains, old Norman battleswords,
robes, and rich French furs,

all are unwrapped and
gloated over, regarded as
tokens of God's love.

From Crécy, from Poitiers,
they return: the black rats
following their Black Prince.

The Lists of Coventry

Then, it was just a means of arbitration,
Ordeal by mass entertainment: two knights,
Like glittering exhibition cases, armed,

Escutcheoned, and embroidered, their chased
Lances quivering at the opposite ends
Of a concourse, waiting for the first trumpet

To send painted Swan and Antelope charging
Down on painted Mulberry Tree and Lion;
Or a more urgent trumpet – like the voice

Of a ten-year-old trying to make himself
Heard above his advisers, above the mob
Writhing around Wat Tyler's corpse – to cry out

'Let me be your leader!', and in a
Kingfisher flash of crimson and green-blue
Velvet, prevent the bloodshed. A lover

Of spectacle, and the colourful arts
Of peace, King Richard stands up to flourish
Words in illuminated filigree

From a goat-hide scroll…and we recollect
That Pathé shot of Chamberlain after Munich;
Or a dark-suited, bespectacled John Nott

Stumbling through the lists of British losses.

Portrait of Henry V by an Unknown Artist

Behind the bodkin nose
and shadowy curve

of occiput
is a draw-weight

of thirteen years,
of which the pursed lips

and brass basilisk
eye are sole evidence:

an eye which, seeing
the French emissary

beg consideration
for twelve thousand

women and children
refugees,

stays blind –
though open, as if

it were looking back-
wards and could sense

the grip of a fist
around the neck's

smug folds, or
a paternal tweak

to that monkish crop –
as if it had long known

the source of its pain,
but longed to glimpse,

further back, the figure
without a crown

drawing his
vengeful bowstring.

Elizabeth Woodville to Edward IV

I remember May Day,
and the maypole
we danced around.

You had told your court
that you were gone
into the country – and O!

we hunted well
that afternoon
in my great bed:

over the ha-ha
and straight into
the chase,

astride, through
your royal forest
we rode, you voracious

for a kill, I
for the sounding
of the mort.

I could not conceive –
crossing the bridge
towards

that sacred altar
to present my sacrifice,
when I saw

such images hanging there
of your beautiful face,
so many Edwards

in tinfoil, winking
and rippling
like the God of Love

above the complaisant
River Thames – that now
I was the Queen

I was a beast
to be taken at
the King's pleasure.

Again it is May Day,
and the maypole
has been erected –

not for me, but for
those 'merriest, wiliest,
and holiest' harlots

that you laughingly
tell me about
as you pass by.

If I had not said
yes when you requested
the rights

of warren in my husband's
bed, Elizabeth
Woodville would

be the Queen of England
truly – the only carcass
there to have eluded you.

Richard III

That King Richard was a child-murderer,
This every child knows.

                    Out on the moors
I first learned not to absorb bitterness
Or let it perish the soul. I was seven,
Had seen my uncle and my brother killed,
My father's head impaled on Micklegate Bar.

That King Richard was a child-murderer...

I learned to deflect my darker instincts
Off a bleak smile, to make a sole companion
Of the moor. Once, let a Jervaulx monk expound
My sinfulness; later, a veteran
Of Agincourt teach me to ride and use
The longbow.

                    That King Richard was a child –
King Richard the Third...

                    When I was thirteen,
I was brought to watch the Woodvilles dancing
My brother, King Edward, to their golden tunes
On the terraces of Greenwich and of Shene.
I suffered their jeers, smiled, but did not see
In their dance how they were already weaving
From the red brier and the white a garth
To trap the truth.

                    That King Richard the Third,
O Tudors...

                    That the pure reputation
I carried south from Wensleydale to share
Was to be adulterated with a butt
Of Malmsey, and two small velvet bundles.

THREE
CIVIL WAR
POEMS

Archie Armstrong to the King

*(Archie Armstrong was Court Jester
to King Charles the First)*

Laughter even in war:
when there is naething
but blude on the air

I hae kept men laughing,
plain men considered
too plain for preserving,

a beldam widowed,
a bairn lost,
I hae seen them all led out

in fits at what I hae tossed
in their direction –
rattling wi' it! Weel...maist

smile a *fraction*...
but mony hae laughed
as they lay their necks on

the block...The others,
who wouldna give in,
but scowled, the buggers,

introverted as sin,
all silent like a poker,
I screeched at 'em: 'Grin,

mon, grin! Life's a joker,
and it's the ane card
that trumps death!' But folk

are daft. Maybe it's hard
for 'em to accept
that heaven might be barred

to Puritans, and kept
braw for Jesters.
It's nae what they expect.

Charles I on Horseback
(Van Dyck)

The King sits rigid, in chalky
bewilderment: his favourite grey
has just trotted calmly through a grove
and into a green morass, been swallowed,
and left him astride a nightmare
whose outline still glares at him, carved white
on that imaginary hillside opposite.

The dark equerry, the smiling equerry,
so quick to come to His Majesty's rescue,
has offered him now a fresh and hugely
muscular mount – more like a boulder
weathered to an approximate horse shape,
its miniature head protruding trimly
from a landscape of burial chambers.

The King tries to laugh – this monster
should be before a plough; or hauling some load
home from harvest; at any rate, securely anchored
against such poundings out of the earth
as have today snatched his best horse from under him –
till a sanguine half-smile rising near the oak
assures him that this is a very tranquil bay.

The dark equerry, the crimson equerry
on whom the King turns his back,
pretends that he must just once more polish
His Majesty's helmet before releasing him;
meanwhile, has concealed a flint or a frog's bone
in the crest, breathing into its restive
royal feathers the ancient Horseman's Word.

Cromwell to His Wife Elizabeth

Here in God's water-meadow
where the sun dips
like a fox's tail
and rises
dripping rich light
to paint the willows, fens,
and meandering River Ouse,
are there not greens enough?

Here with our children;
here with my darling mother,
and your most devoted maid;
here with these good workers,
good stout oxen,
are there not smiles enough,
Elizabeth,

that you pollute
a room of plain white
with oils
of the world's monarchy?

What is it in these proud faces
that has so fascinated you
that you can sacrifice your good sense
to one crown after another?

Is it because you are not a bit proud,
and not at all majestic,
that you feel you have to let
vain shadows of Elizabeth
dance and play
above our scrubbed bed-head?

Or have you heard the Fen
whispering
that I should tear down
one particular face
and replace

his picture with my own –
to hang between your Richard
and your Bolingbroke?

Perhaps it is that you would
like to become Elizabeth
the Second, Elizabeth?

Look at the common people.
Keep your ears muffed and watch them
as they survive in unalleviated flatness.

Now look in your own dear glass,
Elizabeth,
and not at these weak-chinned,
weak-eyed strong men.

THE WINTER JOURNEY

with Jane

If you march your Winter Journeys
you will have your reward, so long
as all you want is a penguin's egg.

APSLEY CHERRY-GARRARD
The Worst Journey in the World

Anyhow draw
This folded message up between
The leaning prisms from me below

W.S. GRAHAM

1

Tonight the sun turns. It's Christmas. It's Easter.
It's a summer seaside holiday – on ice! In the distance
The tide crack groaning. But in here, it's roast
Pemmican and party games – 'a magnificent bust!'

Birdie's donned a funny hat. Bill has an egg
Cherry's opened for the riddle. Through thick specs
He reads it: *Why is the Emperor Penguin*
Like the Kaiser? Outside, the ice cracks.

Because – and Titus pops his toy gun,
Evans does the Lancers, and once again our glasses
Are filled for a Coronation toast. *Because the one* –
(Even Scott smiles, moonlight on a concealed crevasse)

Because the one won't take his colonies off the ice,
And the other won't take his eyes off our – Laughter! Laughter!

                    And the laughter dies.

2

With the Somme yet to leap out from its dark ditch, the lanes
Of England throng with youngsters eager to volunteer
And confront horrific odds; and they'll be sure to be cheered
All the way to their catastrophe. But this will not explain

Why three such thoughtful and supremely sane
Volunteers as Wilson, Bowers, and Cherry-Garrard
Should be off this winter on an egg hunt, prepared
For anything, with little hope of luck, and none of gain.

It's as if they knew Scott's Message to the Public, 'That Englishmen
Can endure hardships, help one another, and meet death
With as great a fortitude as ever in the past,'

As if to superimpose that text above their frozen fingers
In a dramatic poster that will probe the faith
Of would-be heroes more deeply even than Kitchener's thrust.

3

Wilson: perhaps a virtuoso romantic,
Mauve, milk-voiced. The bowed and crystalline
Antarctic was the grand he performed to. Perhaps a saint.
He had a disgust of all impurity. Bill would go to the Pole.

Bowers: short, broad, the plain man, penguin-faced,
Whom the exhaustion, the fear, the misery of frost
Seldom bit – he'd be at the log still, pony-tending, making some list.
He said that Christ had once appeared to him. Birdie would go to the
    Pole.

Cherry-Garrard: a good hard worker, and a perfect brick,
From a distinguished house. Well-heeled and well-liked.
The prose tragedian of the final expedition.
He – perhaps he was too short-sighted – would not be going to the
    Pole,

But would survive the two world wars, and trace his
Own way back, repeatedly, to find those friends' cold faces.

4

The Barrier, and soft snow. We can hardly budge
The sledge-runners. Hard crystal. Could be the Golden
Mile for all the progress after we've hauled
The two loads back and forth along the Barrier edge.

Too much oil, too much equipment! Then you've pulled
Off your fur glove to get a firm grasp. What you haven't
Yet grasped is that it's minus forty-seven
Where your fingers are. But when you come to hold

Your supper-dish...Oh for that plain boiled
Snow, or tea perhaps, and a Huntley and Palmer's
Emergency biscuit! The three of us curled
Around our cups, we almost think nothing can harm us,

That we will be able to survive that soul-
Destroying howl, this cage, the megaton cold.

5

You sweat it. You weep it. You excrete it.
You walk on it. You sleep in it. You eat it.
If you like, you can shake it out, or chuck some heat at it,
But there's still more creeping at your feet.

It's something you learn to live with, ice. To meet it
Halfway. The only time you will escape it
Is at night, when it thaws, when you're asleep.
So long as you're sleeping it will relax that grip.

But you can never sleep, because of the frost,
Because of the fear you won't wake,
Because, like the princess, once you rest
You can't be roused. Only if you're kissed.

But all the kings' sons are either stuck fast
Or outside still hoping the barrier will break.

6

A six-stone, four-foot bird that never sings,
That swims like a porpoise and dresses
Like an impresario; whose prehistoric predecessors
Had scaly claws, himself waving feathered wings

He's never been known to use... that's the one
We're here to collect: the Antarctic Emperor.
It lays its eggs on bare ice just in the windiest corner
As the winter sets in. Everyone else has gone,

Except this foolhardy creature. And the egg
It enthrones between its belly and its feet,
Bill assures us, is packed with scientific meat,
So it's well worth this few weeks' slog –

Difficult though it makes it to distinguish
The Emperors' foolhardiness from that of the English!

C

Ambassadors of 'the Empire on which the sun
Etcetera' where the sun won't even rise!
There were stars. We had the moon. The aurora
At times. But most, the wind cracked its blunder-
Buss of blizzards and knocked all the lights
Out of the sky. It was the darkness, more
Than the cold. Bill's *Time to get up!* Birdie's groan.
Cherry trying to get some use out of his eyes.

When we were bumping through the lower slopes of Terror
Our heels bruised by the sledges as we sped down
Into the complete black, once the cloud broke, and the sky
Signalled three steps ahead with an ice-mirror.
It flashed about a crevasse. We'd been shown
The trap this time. Perhaps we were not alone.

8

AM GOING SOUTH   AMUNDSEN   What if he tried?
We think of Scott and all the others wintering at the Base.
(Shall we go on? *Yes, yes!* they replied.)

Whether or not we do go, he must decide:
If Scott decides we don't go, England loses face.
AM GOING SOUTH   AMUNDSEN   Would he have lied?

And back home, commiseration, criticism, wide
Publicity of our abandoned mission, failure, disgrace...
(Shall we go on? *Yes, yes!* they replied.)

But if we went we'd have the ranks of England's pride
To defend us! If we went, and if we won that race...
AM GOING SOUTH   AMUNDSEN   What if he tried?

(Shall we go on? *Yes, yes!* they replied.)
If we don't go we'll wish we had gone even though we died.

9

To howl. A fit of shivering. Your flame gutters.
At a hundred and ten degrees of frost you feel
Each fresh drop as a fresh turn on the wheel
Of the rack. Like lock-jaw, your body chatters

Till a dream has at last solidified: of your mother's
Arms and of Papa's bookcase, of cook's hot meals,
Of a girl, of girls –
                                But now the Killer Whale's
Black nose has broken the floe. It scatters

The fantasy. To howl! It's the ice has seized
You through your bag, has snatched the dream
You hugged between your belly and your feet
And smashed it. Left you, a foetus, to freeze.

Cherry yawns. Birdie snores. And Bill calls *Time* –
To howl? To die? To get up and eat.

10

A blindfold and a flash of white and you drop
Down down down (oh dear I shall be late) a jerk!
Stiff. You must be dead. My watch, where – ? I expect
That pink-eyed white angora rabbit hopping
Away along the blue-glazed corridor there…*All right?*
There's a jar marked 'orange marmalade', I'll just –
I said are you all right? Fine, but first I must
Just taste this – did you see it? The white – the white…

The crevasse is dark and deep. You can't express
The pressure of your confused faults, only hang stiff
Like the hanged man. There is no handhold
Word, only the rope. You are within the question
Which has no answer. You must let them lift
You, curiouser and curiouser, back up to the blindfold.

11

They swing, they sway, silk curtaining, they flash like swords
Or searchlights, lemon, orange, green,
Whirling in the east. We lay back our heads

And gazed. Exhausted. Incapable of words.
Wagner. Drury Lane. The kinema. An underground train's
Electric flash. Incandescent flickering leads

Opening through the dark. Distant power-lines
At minus fifty. Ice-angels dancing. Will-o'-the-waste
Luring us. The ghosts of the other dead explorers.

We gazed. We were transfixed. Except near-sighted
Cherry, whose lenses were so utterly iced
Up he missed the show! *But wasn't it so boring*

Stuck out there? Deprived of everything Society
Can offer? The bright lights! Didn't you get depressed?

12

Not a snow petrel. Not an albatross or skua.
Nothing in the bare sky ahead but frost. Might there
Perhaps be a penguin? Or are we the three sole survivors of a war.
Something out of Wells. On Mars. Or in somebody else's nightmare.

At home, in the warm, what's a friend?
Someone to drink with, to joke with. On this trek,
That privilege is all you have between your mind
And the ice. He is the Emperor. You are his egg.

If one of us had faltered, he could have cracked
The rest of us. So there was no argument. At worst,
'We reached bedrock' and crawled into our bags
With a dull groan. The weather was all we cursed.

Then laughter. Songs. Obscure faith. And selflessness.
Bill. Birdie. Cherry. Words could not express...

13

Just how utterly exhausted we were,
Until we brought the second sledge when our own prints
Came to seem like humps we had to lift
Each foot across. Even the 'Winterreise'
Tunes freeze, but feet can't stop. Your harnesses
Are bar-lines. The blizzard plays you on.
And though your lips are solid, and your heart-beat's
Too slow, you sing, anything, but it must get you there!

Ein Licht tanzt freundlich before me.
I'll follow, even though it wants to lure me
To the graveyard with Schubert and Wilhelm Müller.
When you're musically hollow, you surrender yourself
To any gaudy beat. *Hinter Eis und Nacht und Graus*
There is a *helles, warmes Haus*. All I desire is delusion.

14

Antarctica House, its windows are whirls
Of bleariness, its furniture is draped white,
The rooms one long chill draught of dark

Closed doors. Occasionally, a sheet unfurls
A stony sheen, or the leads in the tracery light
With a stained aurora, only to sink back to the stark

Domain of silverware, cut glass, and engraved
Mirrors huge as mountain corries. All the clocks
Have stopped, their rotating suns permanently down.

All the beds, though invitingly smoothed,
Are cold, unoccupied. And each of the household nooks,
That flaw with a spider, a beetle, or a mouse...

Even the servants have gone. Then who was it passed
Us in the butler's pantry, that tail-coated ghost?

15

Tea from wickerwork in a Mallows or a Mawson garden.
With the ladies in Brighton luxury or on a Bexhill beach.
Under the Sunningdale pines in a deevie Ford T,
With golf-clubs. On two wheels strumming a ukelele.

Out at a hop. Or at Hove, watching Alletson's
Brief heatwave. On rollerskates down the prom. And at dusk,
Magic lanterns, moonlit menus, Gipsy Love, the Machiche, the
    Galop,
Or a dip, with the ladies. The love beneath the stars. The leaving
    cards.

Smell of melting wax and strawberries, sound
Of champagne and Caruso. Punt-pole sticking. Straw hat
Floats down to Parson's Pleasure, with the ladies,
Mauve and green in the prolonged light, *Che gelida manina*,

That divine, liberty-steeped, easy, golden July
Nineteen-eleven. This rigor. This winter of a July of nineteen-eleven.

16

When Houdini challenges them to bind him head to foot,
Fetter him, snap handcuffs on him under six stout locks,
Then have him screwed into, riveted into a plate-glass box
Filled with water, which is then itself closed in; or put

Into a strait-jacket, wrapped in thick canvas with straps
Of hide and steel buckles, and requests to be hung upside down
From a crane off the top floor of the highest block in town
So he can demonstrate again the ingenuity of his escapes...

There seems to be little to distinguish us. We volunteered
To be thrown into this dark. Asked to be snow-stocked, frost-
Manacled, strapped in harnesses, immobilised.

We chose to battle against the clock for dear life, just to be cheered
And called a hero. And we, like Houdini, boasted
We could escape even frozen in a solid block of ice.

17

There is nothing I would not give to be free of this cold.
No sin I would not commit if only I could slip this dark.
Take the next five years! But let it slam, this cold,
Behind you. Let me enter your warm oblivion, be safely dead.
My hands, if I could move them, would slash God's cold
And willingly sink towards that fire. And if these wet coils of dark
Relaxed and let my eyes see an exit, I'd forsake the angel of cold
And descend rejoicing to the everlasting burning of the dead.

The surface crush. The sastrugi crunch. Your breath's cold
Crackle. No landmark. Noise only and the unending dark.
Dreams of skipping through a beech grove. Fantasies that the cold
Is really heat and the hollow is alive with the dead.
Weak, wondering why we still go on, so almost dead,
With, what's the point, so almost, going on, so almost dead.

18

Three winters one long winter, more hideous
And harrowing than ever man faced. Feet-thick
The ice, where waves, where a waterfall beat quick
Life before. Minute fangs nip your skin, insidious

White devils. As for warmth, to divide the winters,
None till Ragnarök: the sky then will be scorched
As Fenrir, in the east, in Ironwood, watches
The chains be chewed loose and his wolf-monsters

Fall upon the world – the summer world, the world
Of warmth and women – watches them pulverise it
To a permafrost world, of the wind, of the wolf.

Three winters. The first war in the world
I well remember. The sun gone black, an uncle sacrifices
A nephew, a brother his brother, myself myself.

19

Snowed up, 'snow on snow', we sing. Christina's
Bleak winter can't have been a patch on ours.
If she could only have seen these
Three Foolish Men looking for their Emperor's

Nesting place, she might have framed a more
Sardonic sketch of faith: a penguin
Messiah, a pilgrimage to the Source
Of Ornithology, a flock of British bedouin

Following a star called Scott, sanguine,
Single file, in furs and silver, carrying instruments,
Formaldehyde, and a box to put the eggs in.
The frosty wind made a moan like innocence

In agony, and the Selfridges display pane
Was shattered by a jag of terminal moraine.

20

Hammer the bag's fur mouth open, enter for
Your seven-hour stretch on the shark's teeth!
Immortal bird, we've had our beaker full

Of the South! Now for a Waterford decanter
And a tulip glass; moist lips, blushes, breath
Of cinnamon and cloves; mulled metaphor...

I've seen Mount Erebus scrawl hot smoke
In the ice – and though my pencil-lead will freeze
Before it can write the equivalent word, sex

Is at the core, and almost sufficient. A yogi,
Perhaps, could withstand conditions bad as these
By imagining a fire in his solar-plexus,

But we, poor Englishmen, with our endlessly damp fusees,
Haven't the spirit, haven't the will for mystic vestas.

21

To create a home must rank, after sex,
As the most insistent urge. The rite
Of wall-building. To invoke a finite
Motif from the harsh atmospherics

Of atonality, where even your own tracks
Make no development or resolution. We chose a site
Just below the top of the hill, and that same night
Attacked the ice. But even with steel picks

Evolution from the Glacial to the Paleolithic takes
More time than you'd imagine. By hurricane light
We lug boulders, shovel snow, and chip white
Occasional glimpses of home in igloo blocks.

In such an artificial chromatic glow, these might
Well be Cheltenham, Lamer House, H.M.S. Fox.

22

This was the dream, three nights:
One summer
A cold wave had come
And froze the earth to ice.

By the second, Lorraine's
Canals were rigid,
That ruddy-faced wine region
White, still. It came

To the third dream. Cold
Would have killed
All life – but there was a peach tree
With peach-halves in syrup, which I

Reached out to take
And crunched my tongue awake.

23

'The Emperor of the Sorrowful Realm was there:
Out of the encircling ice he stood breast high'
And we stand, drugged by the wind's jab, staring
At the wingless bird that flaps as if to fly,
Or as if to whip what stuns us on our exposed ledge.
A monster: many-faced, multiple-eyed
Emperor of Hell. Each mouth clenched on the legs
Of a sinner. Three at a time. With a piteous sound.

But they are penguins. And we are here for their eggs.
Slither down. Among the addled scraps are found
Three whole shells. Into our mitts
And escape back up the mountain. Looking round,
Thinking to see the head of the Great Lord of Dis,
We saw only those great broken eggs on the ice.

24

Having descended to where, like at the funeral
Of Tolstoy, black pathetic mourners in stiff
Procession wound slowly beneath the cliff
Supporting their precious charge: Imperial
Penguins' eggs; having snatched enough material
For Bill and the B.M. (something to show
For it all) plus fuel for the blubber-stove,
Tonight we ate fresh Emperor! A fitting memorial.

Now all at once we're listening. Some kind of incorporeal
Revenge has begun, starting with a deathly calm.
We are being inspected. A million little crabby claws
Are preparing to devour us. Inside, the cheery old
Atmosphere remains. But outside, the silence has become
Unsustainable. It breathes. It scratches at the door.

25

Our hair must be turning white, our mouths
Are already toothless. Do our heads tilt
On their axes? Magnetic South, True South,
Which? Just wildly spinning? Did the jolt
Unbalance us when we fell from our prams?
Does that explain the indulgent smile whenever friends
Rebuke: you children think your games
In Never-Never-Land will never end?

Near Kirriemuir I first put my plea
To Bill, persuaded him, near Kirriemuir,
To take me to the Pole. Then, the plot
Of the Lost Boys, the Captain, and Peter,
Wasn't in our minds. ('My dear Barrie, we are
Pegging out in a very comfortless spot...')

26

When, with your compartment windows down, on a holiday
Excursion to the coast, you've at last begun to relax
And dissolve with the twin sister giggling of the tracks,
The horses and hills, ploughmen and spires, your express hurls

You all, with two short howls, into a hurricane
Of steam, dumb-smothering you with shrieks
Of grease and wind, wild hysterics,
And a pandemoniacal dark...It was the same

When we were hit, quite unprepared: *Bill! Bill!* –
Like an alarm cord pulled – *the tent has gone!*
Sent us staggering madly into the storm.

We fought. We clawed. We dragged what gear was still
Left out there into our hut. The tent had gone.
The roof next. And finally any hope of our ever getting warm.

27

Our tent. No sooner reappeared than it has become
The Big Top, and we are the trio billed
To tread the high wire, to perform
Above the white wards dim with thrilled
White faces. *Ladies and Gentlemen...*
Don't you feel the ice-fall nudge you off balance?
Steady your mind now. Grip the mental mean
That sways on either side of you across the silence.

This pole, those flurrying eyes, the dark circus
Must go on, in spite of nerves. The nation's
Hush has already volunteered your carcass
For the Great hobbling Push towards an ovation.
Ladies and Gentlemen, from Darkest
Antarctica, the Death-Defying Sensation –

28

For all that optimistic badinage
When we were lashing down crate after crate of provisions,
Pony-fodder, and petrol for the motor-sledges...
Whenever we stopped, our eyes would move to the horizon

In the south, to that fading, defiant image
In gold, like a sovereign whose head attrition
Has reduced to a robe and crown. In an earlier age
One might have even shivered, but the present

Is aware that Halley's comet passes on average
Once in every lifetime. In 1910 it came. It isn't
Expected again till 86. It's not a sign. It doesn't presage.

It simply passes. A wanderer. An icy remainder of fission
In the farthest circle. Yet it set us on edge,
To be seeing it there, and sailing in its direction.

29

'Steadfastly, surely,' said the *Express* Correspondent,
Its twenty thousand tons of nothing slid
'Like some movement of Fate…as a glacier glides
To the sea'…Steel bauble, diversion for the affluent,

A jerry-built toy! From the White Star, Bruce Ismay
Is standing proud and smiling in the dock.
Twenty-two knots, yes sir! he assures us. Nearer New York
To Thee. Blue Riband in his eyes, a smile.

We are still at Crozier, listening to the wind rivet
Its Ross Sea Dreadnought, Unsinkable,
To be sent north next spring, parade tiptoe

In front of millionaires and aristocrats who'll have it
Photographed and still not picture the unthinkable,
The cold, the dark, the seven eighths below.

30

I'm awake at the crack, but not of dawn. Once I woke
To hear the same noise, in February – ponies at the oats,
I thought. Dark then, too. A thin mist. Then this vague rocking,
And, gradually, the long black tongues poking out of the floes

As far as the eye – and Guts had gone! The rest we had to make
Jump, before they'd drifted or slipped off and were swallowed
Into those hideous jaw-crevasses. Again now the creak.
It freezes me in soaked sweat, the heaving groans

Of the pressure-ridge. You expect at any moment the bilious
Motion, the black openings to be licking the split pack,
Your gear sunk, your tent stranded, the corvine killers
Sidling under you…Then the cold coughs: it's winter, relax.

Today you only have to manhaul two huge loads
Through the pitch dark, across concealed crevasses, towards

31

Another time, when there was a lake here, warm
With fish-life, palms round it, emerging species
Struggling out, and before that, before the slopes of beech
And conifer, before the snail even, before the worm,
In earliest Jurassic, when the earth's womb
Was trailing afterbirth and the red screech
Which was life had wriggled, unloved, unleashing
Its wild schemes to expand and overwhelm
Its feverish, exhausted mama – imagine…

And in a couple of million centuries' time,
Us, sitting in our tent atop that blue shining
Mile-deep history of heat and raging
Blizzards, chafing dead limbs at a primus,
On the point of succumbing to evolution.

32

We are caricatures who box between the slits
In the spinning rim of a toy. We are spun
To re-enactment on this wheel, for the fun
Of experiencing continual defeat. Among the exhibits

In the Crystal Palace, beneath the curving lights
With organ and wind-machine, in wax: Birdie,
Cherry, and Bill. The tableau, *Victorian Murderers*
Is next to ours, *Edwardian Suicides*.

There is no getting away, there's little hope
Of ever getting out of this. It was a hazardous
Undertaking. Not heroes, three foolish men.

We are small figures in a crystal globe
Turned upside down and shaken to a blizzard
By a child, who laughs, and shakes it again.

33

'A stranger I came out here, a stranger I go back'
The summer months amused us. We watched the sea-ice crack.
The papers spoke of heroes. Our leader of the Pole.
But now we feel these ice-jaws devour our very soul.

It's every day and all day, or else our fuel won't last.
In darkness, minus seventy, we haul against the blast.
The moon and cloud in conference allot a gleam or two.
A glimpse of guttering footholds, black smudges in the blue.

For God's sake why put up with this? It's going to drive us mad.
Those penguin cries will haunt us. Their eggs will all be bad.
My blank thoughts are irregular. My breath has turned to rhyme.
I'll close my verse behind me, and I may be out some time.

Have cut a final ditty for the public as I walked.
A valedictory spiral. To be sung the way I talked.

34

Glockenspiel, wind-machine, and wordless chorus.
Closer, shuddering the diaphragm, closer time cuts
The groove, records our Sinfonia Heroica.
Glockenspiel, wind-machine, and wordless chorus.

Icicles of string begin the lament in A minor.
We are beneath the knife, we can feel this
Cancer cut from our throats, we have seen into the abyss.
Icicles of string begin the lament in A minor.

A Christian soul from deep within the ice-fall
Summons us. Absurd, our hurdy-gurdy
Tune grinds on: *auf dem Eise*

Wankt er hin und her Go forth upon thy journey
Christian soul, from deep within the ice-fall,
und sein kleiner Teller bleibt ihm immer leer

35

All is well. I shall simply – I have no regret –
I shall simply fall and go to sleep in the snow –
Except in leaving you to struggle through alone –
Mere faith, mere absolute faith that even that
Is all for the best. I'd like to have seen your latest letters.
Dad's little compass and Mother's little comb
Are in my pocket. I had wanted to send news home
But we'll all meet after death, death, death is
All is well. We have struggled to the end. What matters
We have done what we thought was best. My own
Dear wife, goodbye, God be warm to you, blow
Kiss, wind, crack, and a cheer from Cherry: the hut is
Straight ahead. Then have I slept twice sixty-seven miles?
Or Heaven is a hut, hot cocoa, familiar smiles.

36

One day in nineteen-ten I had a fleeting vision.
I saw in imagination a solemn pagan rite,
Sage elders seated in a circle watching
Young men march themselves to death.

One day in nineteen-eleven it was dark
And I heard Corinthians read, and an arrangement
Of St Matthew played to a Coronation March,
My friends pictured in tombs within Westminster.

One day after nineteen-twelve has passed,
The pressure to obey one steadfast finger
Will have crushed my craving for the solitary wastes
Into a pungent relish for adventure

Of any sort, so off to a trench in Flanders.
Es ist nichts als der Winter, es ist nichts als der Winter.

PRIVATE WOODLAND

How safe, methinks, and strong, behind
These trees have I incamp'd my Mind

ANDREW MARVELL

I Still Would Plant My Apple Tree

Last night, the wind blew down the apple tree
We had planted before we were told our world
Might end tomorrow.
                      Today, she sorts through
The seed-packets, extravagant annuals
We always, in the past, shunned in favour of
Some slow-growing, undemonstrative shrub.

I stake the tree. All set for the next gale.
Its branches wear no hint as to whether
There's life within.
                    Three hammer blows
And she calls, 'I'm off to my appointment!'

The blossom is in her face. And her words –
She grips their meaning – cut with a cold edge.

The London Plane

A frost rang early with the results:
Cling, now, to your life's short year, for each
Of its yellowing days must let the five senses

Twist, then drop, until you are naked asleep.
Awake – patched, yet with hardly a wrinkle –
You stretch and bend to shade the truth from us,

But must submit, an ashen almost-skeleton,
To be avenued in soot-free, showerless white,
Falling in with these others, octogenarians also –

Survivors of the repeated spring raids,
Hawkers of a century's detritus, Londoners –
Londoners to your lacewood core!

Allow, gradually, the soft expansion from beneath
That rigid bark to shuck whatever poverty
Or close-grained prejudice could not resist.

Hug your next year's buds. Accept
And protect the swelling in the hollow stem
Of each hour, each last breath, until the day falls.

Walnuts

She would plant two saplings.

There would be silence from the burial place,
but in the future, each Christmas,
home-grown walnuts.

             As if a word
picked green had then gone sour,
she flinched – these family crackings
the exposed ends of a nerve-tree.

A figure deep in the pickling jar.
Two daughters coolly hooking brain from skull.
A father and a mother trying to split
their wrinkled shells.

             There would be silence.
There would be years of fruitlessness.

She would plant two walnuts.

The Oak

Approaching the perimeter, the boy
Who dreams of 'Down the Bright Stream', and the man
Who knows 'Guernica'. The boy who will ask
What oak apples are, and the man who won't
Explain that they are tumours. The boy who hopes
To spot a red squirrel. The man who says
They will all prove grey.
                              My childhood and I
May never have danced Hey Derry Down as
Our forefathers danced around the oak, but
We have learnt to read the signs that tell us
THESE WOODS ARE PRIVATE.
                              Thick arteries
Have thickened until they shiver behind
This ragged blanket. Young companies
Of hazel that wriggle their golden tassels
In a lithe floorshow fascinate and stir
The man. The boy looks up at a jigsaw sky.

A Wicked Witch, The Thunderer, or a Phantom?
The words on the wire repeat their one sound.
These woods, These woods – like a stock dove begging –
These woods have danced a navy on their knees,
Are War Office Property and have been
Since the Ice Age, since the first battering rams.
Five hundred varieties of riddle
And song: the woodpecker attack, plain cuckoo,
Or a brace of Cruise. These woods are private,
And since we can read, we shall not trespass.

But words have not yet heard of literacy.
Outlaws, half wild, they will flee with Rimbaud
To the forest, hide there, seem to have helped
Manoeuvre your woolly thoughts into a pen –
But then leap out at you, tear at your heart.
They'll not come to your knife, but screech and squeal
Like sawmills to be fed.

                    Robin Hood's Larder.
The Royal Oak. The Parliament Oak.
The Oak of William the Conqueror, and
Harry's Oak. Oaks that were pulpits.
Oaks that were gibbets. Oaks that are jokes and
Resemble naked men. The oak that Hitler
Gave to a Public School. The haunted oaks.
The stranded oaks. The oak of the artist
Or poet. The commemorative oaks.
And oaks strapped round for forty feet of circumference
That simply sprang up wild from a roadside hedge.
The oak that was an acorn on an oak
That grew as Christ grew.
                              These words are public
And this side of the perimeter fence.
There have been songs to which no creature knows
The words and words which nothing – not the raven
On Odin's shoulder, not the writing-desk
Veneered like the chart of a distant sound –
Can solve.

            Pieces indistinguishably blue.

Gathered where they dropped but cannot germinate,
Brought to the open, free of history,
Free of the long shadow, they may be saved
From extinction, which is in every cup.

The Ash

the Ash is for you

because of its charcoal buds
because it conceals white magic
because it can hold all winter
creation's keys

because it is tough

because as a spear, a hoop,
a chess-set, a picture-frame,
or a stage brace
it will keep its elasticity

because it can make its own face up

first appearing with ruddy mountain cheeks
then in pale chorus
weeping through Twickenham gardens

then the scarred and grizzled hero
of some grey Norse epic

collapsing
to a sudden curtain

because it is like a chameleon
an old Polonius

because it can smile
heal advertise
mesmerise
and tell tall stories

because it was once Yggdrasil
because it is
the last of the species in our end game
Jack, the Ash is for you

Sweet Chestnut

Maturity is to know the star-shakes
in your heart. It is to have turned aside

and, despite the upright and the smooth, gone on
turning. It is to be twisting free of

one's roots, ascending to its very lip
the twin helix. To have observed each year

some fresh disfiguring lump. To have felt
the next ring splitting under the renewed weight

of spring. It is to have seen the spears
lifted, then a spiked mace.

On slopes of ash to have faced the eruption
of your griefs. To have flowered. To propagate.

Loveliest of Trees
(for Katie: b. 16 May 1986)

Cherry Ward
in mid-May –

one waste corner
of our lives

is suddenly
in blossom and

we are laden
with this puckered

and purple fruit,
a basketful

of sweet Katie,
bitterly loved

by us, and
by the birds.

Cuckoo
cherry tree

come down
and tell me

how many years
she has to live.

Beechwood
(for Jürgen Sandmann)

Yes, it's a lifetime. But the complexions
Are no less smooth, the trunks, the rigidity
Of salute, proclaim no less their mastery.
Those dead – how can you shake them off? Not here,
Marching the ABC of a beechwood trail.
In the picnic areas, the birds still
Sing 'Horst Wessel'. The soft insignia
Of the beech-nut is still cast into spiked
VW's, row upon row of steel bonnets.
Nor have the altar carvings (the swastika,
Heart, or star) grown out; but have become sealed
Into boles huge as cathedral buttresses.
Not even the annual Landschaftswunder,
Printing a spring, manufacturing a youth,
Can quite dislodge that crumpled rattle
Of Billionmarkscheine. Or these roots
That, on our nature trek, catch and hold you
Like an Aramaic hand, untraceable.

SONNETS
FOR EUROPE

White Cliffs

Whistling round into Shakespeare Cliff, where poor
Mad Tom led his blind father to the verge
Of devotion, my only daughter saw
From the carriage window the darkness surge
In upon her. I comfort her with talk
Appropriate to her three months of light,
Sweet nothings such as King Lear perhaps once spoke
To his beloved fool, before the night
Tunnelled his wits. Still she will not settle.
I would have tried to lull her with that long
Blank verse speech of Edgar's if I thought beetle,
Chough, or crow talked peace. But she wants a song,
So: 'There'll be bluebirds over...' Searchlights sweep
Above these black white cliffs, and she's asleep.

Borders

We cross borders, and don't even get out
Our passports now, as if these mapped frontiers
Were a well-healed scar: after all, it's years
Since there was anything to fight about
In Europe – brownshirts, the uniformed lout
Who looked you in the eye until your tears
Ran cold, these are gone; here, no-one disappears
Except to snatch a wurst and sauerkraut
In the autobahn café. Yet if you've read
Or heard tales, or seen newsreels of the war,
You will want to know the faces of those who
Crossed this line before you and are dead,
Who were startled by an early knock at the door,
Or picked out from some shuffling exit queue.

Chagall Windows
(Mainz)

Chagall, the ninety-year-old, from deep shades
Of love, transfiguring the Scriptures to a blue
Glass covenant, that Gentile might live with Jew,
Paints unaware of the post-war parade
Outside St Stephan's, where retired ladies
And gentlemen of Mainz patiently queue
In front of a plate-glass shop-front for new
Special offers, and do not seem afraid
Of sudden reflections; of Kristallnacht
Winking at them; of a myriad store-
Windows smashed in hatred; of glimpsing back through
That stark proscenium to the final act...
Paints unaware that they will claim they saw
Nothing, their eyes clear, and glazed Chagall-blue.

Im Schwarzwald

Deep in the Black Forest lie Germany's rich
Resources of myth – 'im Schwarzwald' – a place
Untouched by man, far from the lemming-race
Of business lunches, saving schemes, and kitsch.
It is the land of fairy-tales, of scritch-
Owl moonlit nights when you might almost trace
A hill-top's name back to its source, to a face
From your own dreams, earth-mother, elf, or witch.
And it is not here that the summer showers
Have begun to acidulate the trees,
Not from here that the common alpine flowers
Are vanishing along with birds and bees.
The nymphs will never leave these sacred bowers.
Nor is there caesium dust upon this breeze.

The Jungfrau

You didn't come for Jung, but for the Jungfrau.
Stout wooden bridges crossed tumultuous streams
To a Centre where you could have had your REM-
Sleep frozen and dissected and learnt how
To read that faint melancholy rainbow
Arched between this morning mist and the beams
In last night's zigzag mountain-pass, your dreams
Laid open for repair. But it's too late now –
The streams have broken the wooden bridges
And the woman without a face is sleeping
Nude in your hotel bed again, the view
Exactly as you desired: cold ridges
Of consummation, and the guilt creeping
Too slowly to be seen, but towards you.

Verdun

Needles have put these battle-wounded hills
Into a deep sleep: innumerable shots
Of darkness have calmed the nightmares that wailed
Through this landscape by day. Conifer roots
Do not need topsoil, will conceal flesh and bones,
And grow so quickly their branches can catch a phrase
From music-hall and conceal it until it keens
Like a low wind. Conifers can erase
Almost everything – warm limbs or cold steel,
Craters, corpses, barbed-wire, a rusted machine-
Gun, a head, a heart, an unexploded shell –
Almost everything, to a profound green,
While the fruits that have kept these comatose hills
Alive, drop in handfuls like sleeping pills.

The English Dream

The English dream of nothing as grimy
As a coal-mine, but of a filigree past,
Nothing as real as a steel industry –
They would prefer to do without the last
Two hundred years and live in a century
They imagine to have been, where good taste
Was a knot garden, not a chip factory.
Revolutions can change too much too fast...
So we sit, and we soak up glossy brochures
Touching the gilded realms of William Morris;
In easy chairs hand-wrought from English oak,
Leafing through woods and streams and air as pure
As celluloid, where shepherds woo Chloris
With ingenious rhymes, and there's no work.

Repatriation
(December 1989)

We who have withstood raids by dragon-boats
And cowered in thatched mud camps while a fire-storm
Flayed our perimeter fence – seen our warm
Fleeces bled, drinking-holes spiked, ash threshed from oats...
We who once clung, through years of salt, to remote
Salvages and a dream of syrup trees,
And learnt, at the first breaker, refugees
Should never dream...Who took the strain when notes
From expeditionary gulls gybed our throats
To a raw haven, without homes or work,
No new world, but a crossing from Dunkirk
In open pleasure cruisers...We who loved boats
Must now push these people into the air!
Who will rescue us from our raft of votes?

John Greening was born in 1954 and brought up in Hounslow on the outskirts of London. He studied at Swansea, Exeter, and Mannheim Universities, then tried his hand at various jobs – including that of children's conjuror – before joining Radio Three as Hans Keller's Clerk, New Music. He married in 1978 and he and his wife spent two years on Voluntary Service Overseas in Aswan, Upper Egypt. *Westerners*, his first book of poetry and one of the many fruits of that tour, was published by Hippopotamus Press in 1982. After teaching Vietnamese Boat People in Arbroath for eighteen months, and receiving a Scottish Arts Council Writer's Bursary, he and his wife settled in Huntingdonshire, where their first child was born. He now teaches English at Kimbolton School. In 1990-91 he spent a year teaching in America on a Fulbright exchange.

John Greening's poems have been published widely in leading literary magazines, and in 1988 he was a top prize-winner in the Arvon/*Observer* International Poetry Competition judged by Ted Hughes and Seamus Heaney. He won first prize in the Alexandria International Poetry Festival in 1981. His short stories have appeared in various anthologies, including Peter Ackroyd's *P.E.N. New Fiction* (Quartet), and he has written stage plays about Robert Louis Stevenson and Oliver Cromwell.

The Tutankhamun Variations (Bloodaxe Books, 1991), his second book, contains six sequences, four historical and two contemporary.